W9-BZW-282

THE LIBRARY OF
AMERICAN
LIVES AND TIMES™

NATHAN HALE

Patriot and Martyr of the American Revolution

L. J. Krizner
Lisa Sita
THE NEW-YORK HISTORICAL SOCIETY
BPMS
Media Center

The Rosen Publishing Group's
PowerPlus Books™
New York

To my parents, Bob and Marianne Krizner —L. J. Krizner

To the kids: Tonie, Ricky, Stephanie, Matthew, Joey, Sean, Lisa, Patrick, Bianca, Gabriella, and Julia —Lisa Sita

The authors wish to thank Stewart Desmond, Phil Leahy, and Richard Mooney for their contributions to this book.

Published in 2002 by The Rosen Publishing Group, Inc.
29 East 21st Street, New York, NY 10010

First Edition

Editor's Note: All quotations have been reproduced as they appeared in the letters and diaries from which they were borrowed. No correction was made to the inconsistent spelling that was common in that time period.

Library of Congress Cataloging-in-Publication Data

Krizner, L. J.
Nathan Hale, patriot and martyr of the American Revolution / by L. J. Krizner and Lisa Sita.— 1st ed.
    p. cm. — (The library of American lives and times)
Includes bibliographical references and index.
  ISBN 0-8239-5724-1
1. Hale, Nathan, 1755–1776—Juvenile literature. 2. United States—History—Revolution, 1775–1783—Secret service—Juvenile literature. 3. Spies—United States—Biography—Juvenile literature. 4. Soldiers—United States—Biography—Juvenile literature. [1. Hale, Nathan, 1755–1776. 2. Spies. 3. United States—History—Revolution, 1775–1783—Secret service.] I. Sita, Lisa, 1962– II. Title. III. Series.
  E280.H2 K75 2002
  973.3'85—dc21
                                                          2001000601

Manufactured in the United States of America

CONTENTS

1. The Martyr Patriot

Nathan Hale was only twenty-one years old when, on a Sunday morning in September, the British hanged him as an enemy spy. It was 1776, and the American colonies were fighting the Revolutionary War for independence from Britain. Young Hale was already a captain in the Continental army. The American soldiers, poorly trained and without proper supplies, were battling against a powerful force. The British army was made up of highly trained, professional military men backed by a strong navy whose ships were anchored offshore. Fighting the British was a difficult and often disheartening challenge for the American army. In the summer of 1776, General George Washington was stationed in New York with his troops, who were badly outnumbered by the British. Washington needed an able man to go behind the British lines on Long Island and secretly gather information about what the British were planning to do next.

Opposite: This undated, hand-colored engraving shows Captain Nathan Hale. Though he died early in the Revolutionary War, his name and legacy as a great American hero live on.

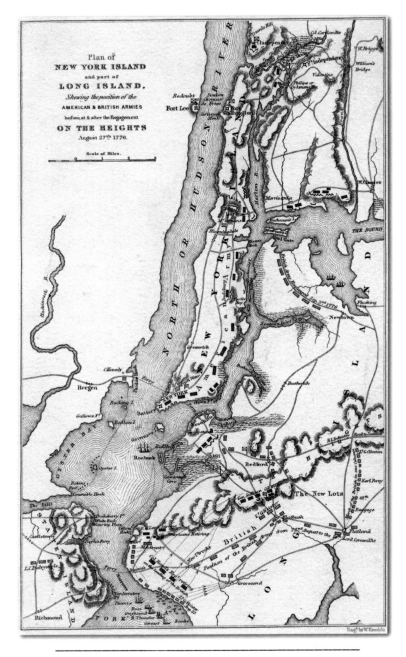

This is a plan of New York and part of what used to be Long Island, showing the positions of the American and British armies before, during, and after the Battle of Long Island near Brooklyn Heights, on August 27, 1776. On about September 16, the American army retreated and camped in Harlem Heights, and Nathan Hale sneaked behind enemy lines on Long Island.

Nathan Hale volunteered for this dangerous mission. On his way back to safety, after having completed his task in the British camps, he was captured and executed.

Nathan Hale is sometimes known as a martyr, or someone who willingly suffers, and often dies, for his or her beliefs. Hale was a martyr patriot because he sacrificed his life for the cause of American freedom, remaining true to his principles right up to his death. According to one of his sergeants, Stephen Hempstead, "Captain Hale was one of the most accomplished officers, of his grade and age, in the army . . . young, brave, honorable . . . he suffered for his country's sake." But who was this courageous young man so eager to undertake a secret and risky mission?

Hale was a scholar as well as a soldier. Born in Coventry, Connecticut, he graduated from Yale College. Before joining the army, he was a schoolteacher and one of the few people of his day to support the education of women. Nathan was liked and admired by those who knew him. An honest, trustworthy, and friendly person, he was also energetic, athletic, and full of patriotic enthusiasm. When Washington, urgently needing help, called for a volunteer to slip behind enemy lines, Hale offered himself. He knew the risk: If he was caught, he would be killed. Yet his sense of duty made it impossible for him to refuse, even when friends tried to convince him not to go.

Some of the people who died in the war for independence are remembered for their extraordinary deeds.

What is a spy? According to the rules of war, a spy is someone who enters into enemy territory, in disguise, to gather information that can be used against the enemy. A soldier in his own uniform who does this is not a spy. A spy performs his duty pretending to be someone he is not. If caught while behind enemy lines, the spy can be executed. If he makes it back to his own side and is then captured, he must be treated as a regular prisoner.

Hale's accomplishments as a soldier were not extraordinary, yet today he is one of the best-known men of his time. Spying was a common practice for both the American and the British armies during the Revolution. Although Hale was an admirable soldier and officer, Hale's spy mission was unsuccessful. In disguise, he had walked bravely into the British camps and had taken notes on all he saw and heard. Yet he was captured, and Washington never received the information gathered. How can a failed spy be a national hero? A closer look at his life and times may help answer this question and show how Nathan Hale came to take his hallowed place in American history.

2. Growing Up in Connecticut

Nathan was born in the beautiful rural colony of Connecticut on June 6, 1755, to parents from two highly regarded New England families. His father, Richard Hale, deacon of his church and a leader of the community, came to Coventry, Connecticut, from Newbury, Massachusetts, in 1746. There he married Elizabeth Strong, and together they had twelve children. Nathan was the sixth. Connecticut was rich with fertile soil, good for farming. Earlier, in the 1600s, ministers had led their congregations to settle the area. Richard Hale followed and became a successful farmer.

Richard and Elizabeth were strict parents. They were devout followers of the Puritan faith, which influenced all areas of their lives. The Puritan devotion to God carried over into education, business, and other social activities. Like many Americans at the time, the Hale family viewed preachers and ministers as God's servants, chosen by Him to guide the community. They also believed that a person could make a better life through hard work and perseverance. The Hales raised

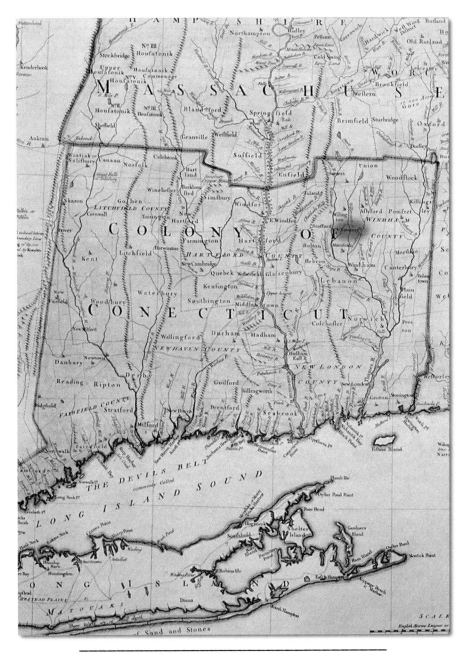

This eighteenth-century map shows the colony of Connecticut, where Nathan Hale grew up. Connecticut was mostly wilderness with some small towns and farms that had been settled by families like the Hales. Richard Hale and his family settled in Coventry, Connecticut, highlighted in purple above.

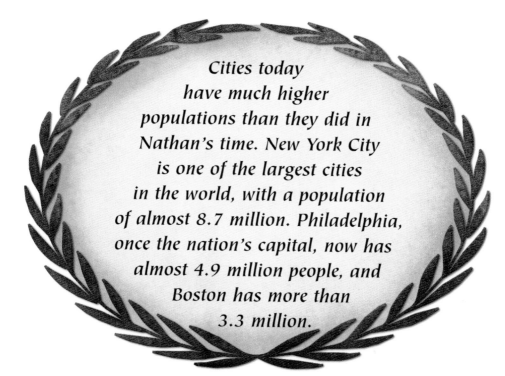

Cities today have much higher populations than they did in Nathan's time. New York City is one of the largest cities in the world, with a population of almost 8.7 million. Philadelphia, once the nation's capital, now has almost 4.9 million people, and Boston has more than 3.3 million.

their family to trust in God, but also encouraged the children to work hard to reach their goals. Richard Hale held education in the highest regard. He made certain that his children received both religious and intellectual guidance and nourishment.

When Nathan was born, America was mostly wilderness. Britain controlled thirteen colonies on the east coast. France had colonies to the north in Canada, as well as other territories in America, and Spain controlled Florida. Most of the British colonists lived in small villages, or on working farms, like the Hales did. There were only a few thriving cities. Philadelphia had about 20,000

BPMS
Media Center

This 1755 map shows the British and French colonial territories
in North America. Orange areas were British territories and green
areas were French territories. The pink area was disputed territory.
The two nations fought the French and Indian War in 1754, to settle
these land disputes. The end of the war brought about new taxes that
would lead to the Revolutionary War during Nathan Hale's time.

people, and Boston and New York each had about 16,000. New York was growing rapidly. Newport, Rhode Island, and Charleston, South Carolina, each had about 10,000 people. A rough and bumpy road connected New York and Philadelphia, passing through rich forests. People traveled by foot, horseback, stagecoach, or boat.

In his first year, Nathan was sickly. In the 1700s, doctors were scarce and illness was not well understood. Medicines we know today, such as penicillin, did not exist. Because of this, many children never lived to be adults, and parents had great cause for concern when children became ill. Fearing that Nathan would die, Richard and Elizabeth watched over him closely. Soon Nathan became stronger. By his second year, he had become a sturdy and healthy boy. He grew to be energetic and active, with a strong, agile body. He loved nature and being outdoors. He especially enjoyed games and sports and was an excellent athlete. He would spring and glide with the ease of a gazelle and was a fine swimmer. All of this was remarkable for a child whose parents had feared he would die as a baby.

Not only was Nathan a fine athlete, he had a thirst for knowledge and studied hard. His father believed he would become a good Christian minister. Nathan's pastor, Reverend Doctor Joseph Huntington, who tutored him in ancient Greek and Latin, also believed Nathan was destined to be a minister. Ministers were some of the most well-educated, influential, and respected members of

This photo from the 1800s shows the First Congregational Church in Coventry, Connecticut. The Hales worshiped at this church. Near the graveyard, where his family members are buried, there is a monument to Nathan Hale.

their communities. In 1769, at age fourteen, Nathan entered Yale College with his brother Enoch, who was two years older. At the time, Yale specialized in preparing young men for the ministry through disciplined classes in religion and the classical languages. Students could also choose to be trained in other occupations, such as law or business. All lessons were in Latin.

At Yale, Nathan was exposed to the new thoughts of the time. The college was not far from Boston and New York, two of the largest colonial cities. Just like cities today, colonial cities served as centers of trade, business, and news for surrounding communities. Cities were also the centers for government.

While Nathan was growing up, the American colonies were part of the British Empire. Each of the thirteen colonies had a governor appointed by King George III. There was no organized way for the colonies to meet to discuss their complaints against George III or Parliament, the British legislature. Each colony dealt directly with the Crown. The colonies were not represented in Parliament.

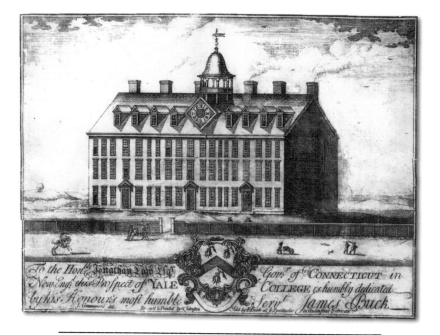

To the Honble Jonathan Law Esqr
New Eng^d this Prospect of YALE
by his Honour's most humble

Govr of CONNECTICUT in
COLLEGE is humbly dedicated
Servt James Buck

This engraving of Yale College is thought to date from 1749.
Nathan Hale would attend Yale with his brother Enoch in 1769.
The college was originally founded as Connecticut College
in 1717, but it was renamed after Elihu Yale in 1718,
when he donated a large sum of money to the school.

The eighteenth century, or the 1700s, was an era of new developments in science and technology. These developments influenced the way many people around the world viewed themselves. American colonists were also beginning to think about themselves in new ways, and had begun discussing new forms of government. They wanted to participate in the decision-making process of their government. They did not want a king making their laws without their approval. They wanted more control over their property and interests.

This eighteenth-century painting of King George III was created by Thomas Gainsborough. George III was born in 1738. He ruled Britain during the American Revolution and wished to keep the colonies under control. In 1811, rule was given to his son. Due to a disease called porphyria, George III died blind, deaf, and insane on January 29, 1820.

Newspapers and pamphlets from Boston made their way to New Haven, bringing ideas about reform and release from the rule of a faraway king. The Hales, father and sons, liked what they heard. They were committed to a government ruled by the people. Both Nathan and Enoch joined a secret literary fraternity, and Nathan became its librarian. The fraternity met weekly in students' rooms, where its members discussed science and literature, and issues such as the ethics of slavery.

At Yale, as in his childhood, Nathan Hale was extremely outgoing. He participated in debates and plays, and was admired by students and tutors, enjoying a full social life. He was always a welcome visitor in the homes of New Haven families. Dr. Aeneas Munson, whose home he visited frequently, described him this way:

> *"He was almost six feet in height, perfectly proportioned, and in figure and deportment he was the most manly man I have ever met. His chest was broad; his muscles were firm; his face wore a most benign expression; his complexion was roseate; his eyes were light blue and beamed with intelligence; his hair was soft and light brown in color and his speech was rather low, sweet, and musical. His personal beauty and grace of manner were most charming. Why, all the girls in New Haven fell in love with him . . ."*

This is a hornbook from colonial times.

During colonial times, young students did not have textbooks. Instead, they used "hornbooks." The hornbook looked like a small paddle, a flat piece of wood with a handle. It hung from a student's neck by a string. A paper attached to the wood was printed with the alphabet, numerals, and stories and prayers from the Bible, such as the Lord's Prayer. This paper was covered by a thin, clear sheet of cow's horn. The hornbook was used to teach reading, but it also enabled teachers to instruct students in the importance of good behavior through the biblical lessons printed on it.

Nathan Hale left his mark on Yale. He became well known for his interest in reading and his physical skill. He graduated with highest honors in 1773. At graduation, he participated in a formal debate on the topic: "Whether the education of daughters be not without any just reason, more neglected than that of our sons." Nathan Hale would revisit this topic—the lack of education for women—once he left Yale College and began his career.

This is the Yale graduation broadside from 1773. It lists the names of the students who graduated from the school in that year, including Enoch and Nathan Hale.

3. The Beginnings of Revolt

Nathan Hale was eighteen years old when he graduated from college. As was customary, his first job was teaching school. Teaching gave Hale an opportunity to make a living while deciding what to do with his professional life. He started teaching in East Haddam, Connecticut, far from the stimulation of the Yale campus in New Haven. Hale missed his friends and their exciting discussions. He was thrilled a few months later when the notable Union School in the seaport town of New London hired him.

Nathan Hale liked New London, which had a newspaper and people eager to discuss the ideas of the time, including resistance to British rule. He taught more than thirty boys reading, writing, mathematics, Latin, and Greek. Students were taught in Latin and English. They learned mainly by memorizing and reciting. Churches controlled education, and discipline was strict. In colonial times, only boys were permitted to go on to higher levels of education. Although both boys and girls were educated at the elementary level, most girls were taught at home

This is the schoolhouse in East Haddam, Connecticut, where Nathan Hale had his first teaching job. In Hale's time, schools were very different from what they are today. All classes were taught in one or two rooms, and children were not separated based on age.

rather than attending a formal school. Even when formal schools did admit girls, very few allowed study for young women past the elementary level. Girls were also taught different subjects from boys, whose education was geared towards the classics, science, and mathematics. Girls were instructed in religious and practical matters, such as correct manners and behavior, as well as reading and writing. They were not taught Latin and Greek. Children of wealthy families had tutors at home, and boys were sometimes sent to England for college.

Nathan Hale was different from most men at that time. He believed in an educated and enlightened society of both men and women. In 1774, he had the idea of holding summer classes for young women, to teach them the same subjects boys learned. This was a bold idea for the time, yet it was in keeping with the progressive social ideals Hale learned in college. The administrators of the Union School agreed, and decided that girls could attend Hale's schoolhouse from five to seven in the morning.

In late 1774, the Union School encouraged Nathan to continue teaching, and offered him a permanent position.

This is the restored schoolhouse in New London, Connecticut, where Nathan Hale accepted a job in 1773. Originally located at Union and State Streets, it has since been moved and now sits at the foot of State Street across from Union Railroad Station.

He enjoyed teaching, and the students and parents treasured his gentle manner. He had done well, and his headmaster took note. Nathan Hale thought long and hard about the job offer. He had always thought he would become a minister but decided to take the teaching position. The families of New London were delighted. Nathan's time in New London had been happy and comfortable. The job offered the challenges he wanted in a career. Just as it had at Yale, his warm personality gained him solid friendships among the town's families. He also continued several close friendships with Yale classmates. As a young adult, the topic he and his friends were most interested in was the worsening situation between the colonists and England. The seeds of war had been sown much earlier, though, when Nathan Hale was only a boy.

New Englanders had been talking about the idea of resisting British rule for some time. Hale's own family believed passionately in the rights of the colonists. After 1763, colonists began questioning Britain's actions toward America. That year, Britain and France signed the Treaty of Paris, ending the French and Indian War. For many years, between 1754 and 1763, Britain and France had been at war in Europe, as well as in North America, where both countries had colonies. Both European countries understood the importance of North America and wanted control over its land and resources. Britain eventually won the struggle for the colonies when all of France's American colonies, called New

This undated engraving shows the 1755 defeat of General
Edward Braddock in the French and Indian War. Braddock and
his men were on their way to capture Fort Duquesne in Pennsylvania,
but were surprised by French and Indian troops. Braddock was
wounded and died a few days later. Both the British and the
French were fighting over land rights in America. Despite what
the name of the war implies, both sides had Indian allies.

France, surrendered. This included much of the eastern
coast of present-day Canada and the land between the
Appalachian Mountains and the Mississippi River.
During the war, Spain had sided with France. When
Britain won, they also acquired Florida from Spain.

Now Britain controlled nearly half of North America
and was responsible for many people, including French
Canadians and American Indians. Britain was also
responsible for protecting these new lands from further
attacks by the Indians and French who still lived on the

land. It cost a lot of money to keep troops in America. The war had also left Britain with huge debts. Britain thought the colonists should help pay for the war and protection from enemies. That meant taxes. To ensure that the taxes were being paid, Britain passed a series of laws, called acts. They began with the Sugar Act of 1764, which required colonists to pay a tax on molasses. In 1765, British parliament passed the Stamp Act. The Stamp Act required the colonists to pay tax on all legal and commercial paper, including pamphlets, newspapers, and almanacs. Each paper required a tax stamp. Parliament set up an agency in the colonies to sell the stamps and

These are examples of the stamps that the British government required to be purchased and attached to printed goods sold in the American colonies.

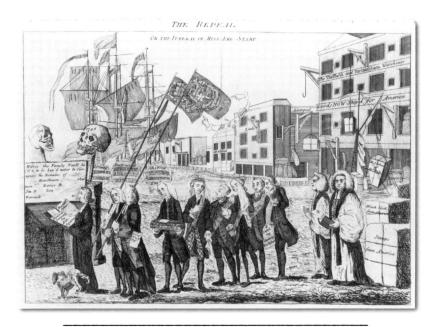

This cartoon was published in a London paper on the day the king repealed the Stamp Act. The cartoon made fun of First Lord of the Treasury George Grenville, here called George Stamper, for this and other unpopular taxes. Grenville carries a small coffin holding his child, the Stamp Act. The two banners being carried by his supporters represent the parliamentary votes against the act.

enforce the law. Although taxes had been placed previously on goods imported to and exported from the colonies, the Stamp Act was the first tax within the colonies. If Parliament could enforce this tax, could they also impose tax on property and other possessions? It was taxation without representation. Many colonists believed this to be tyranny. People did not believe Parliament should determine these laws from across the ocean, where no one spoke on the colonists' behalf. Many colonists felt that Britain had too much power. Revolt was in sight.

The Hales, as well as many other colonists, felt that paying taxes to the Crown without proper representation was unfair. Yet merchants who depended on trade with England did not want to cause a fuss and risk upsetting business. Other colonists wanted no more bloodshed after the French and Indian War. These differences began to divide the colonists. Britain's attempt to tax the colonists led some to discuss resisting the British government. The first whispers of "independence" were heard. People who supported resistance to Britain were called Whigs, or patriots. Those that remained true to the Crown were Tories, or loyalists. Nathan Hale and his family were patriots. They believed that it was their God-given right to prosper, and that they were entitled to wealth, land, and education. They thought that a government that limited this possibility should be defied.

The colonists did not accept the British tax without a fight. Many refused to obey the Stamp Act. Because the colonists had no representatives in Parliament, they called a protest meeting of their own, with representation from all thirteen colonies. It was called the Stamp Act Congress. Nine colonies sent delegates and the others sent word, approving the meeting and agreeing to abide by the decisions made there. The Congress composed a written protest against the tax and sent it to London, and it worked! Britain removed the tax. At the meeting, the delegates also decided to organize a boycott of British-made goods. Many colonists joined in, refusing

THE BOSTONIANS PAYING THE EXCISE-MAN OR TARRING & FEATHERING
Copied on stone by D.C. Johnston from a print published in London 1774 ─── Lith of Pendleton Boston 1830

This print by D. C. Johnston, entitled *The Bostonians Paying the Excise-Man or Tarring and Feathering*, was published in London in 1774. In protest against the new taxes, American patriots tar and feather the exciseman, while, in the background, men dump tea into Boston Harbor. Notice that the Stamp Act tacked to the Liberty Tree is hung upside down to symbolize the colonists' protests against it.

to buy anything from Britain. The organized resistance had begun.

Meanwhile, in Boston, Samuel Adams founded a secret society called the Sons of Liberty. The Sons of Liberty included a range of people, such as bakers, dockworkers, butchers, farmers, and lawyers. Adams, a merchant and brewer, was a great leader in the resistance. The Sons of Liberty all had one thing in common: They opposed British rule. The Sons of Liberty showed their disapproval of the Stamp Act by rioting, destroying tax stamps, tarring and feathering tax collectors, and hanging them in effigy. While some people believed the Sons of Liberty were too forceful, local units sprang up all over, pledging to come to one another's aid if Britain threatened military attack.

It was in Boston that resistance first boiled over into violence. Because of rioting against the Crown, Britain posted troops there to keep watch. British soldiers often lived in the homes of Bostonians, both patriots and Tories, and this increased the tension. On March 5, 1770, some boys began throwing snowballs at the British soldiers. In the commotion, a group of men and boys began to threaten the soldiers with sticks, clubs, and stones. Captain Thomas Preston, a British officer, brought in more soldiers to try to quiet the mob, and the crowd attacked them. The British soldiers fired into the crowd. Three people were killed and eight more were wounded, two of whom died later. The event became

In 1783, after the Revolution,
America consisted of the thirteen
original colonies. It would take decades
for the country to grow to fifty states.
In 1803, the Louisiana Purchase
instantly doubled the size of the country,
thrusting America on the road to expansion.
President Thomas Jefferson bought
the Louisiana Territory, which stretched
from the Mississippi River to the
Rocky Mountains, from the French.
(It was named Louisiana after the French
king, Louis.) Jefferson's main goal in
purchasing the territory was to own
New Orleans, the city that lay at the mouth
of the Mississippi River and that
controlled this major waterway of business.
Jefferson shocked the American people
with the purchase's extravagant
$15 million price tag. In 1804,
Jefferson sent two young explorers,
Meriwether Lewis and William Clark,
to uncover the mysteries that the West then held.

known as the Boston Massacre. This event caused Boston's citizens to call a town meeting and demand the removal of all British troops from the city. The people also wanted to try Captain Preston and his men for murder. John Adams, a patriot who would later become America's second president, was one of the lawyers for the accused British soldiers. Although it was a bold move for a patriot to represent a British soldier in court, especially dur-

This engraving was created by Paul Revere in March 1770. The picture served as a powerful propaganda piece, making the British soldiers appear organized and calculating. In reality they were in chaos as the mob threatened them. Revere also added the sign "Butcher's Hall" above the customshouse to make the colonists even angrier.

ing these tense times, John Adams said, "Council ought to be the very last thing that an accused Person should want in a free Country." He felt that, British or American, it was important to remind the people that laws needed to be respected and followed. Adams believed that it was necessary ". . . to lay before [the people of Boston], the Law as it stood, that they might be apprised of the Dangers . . . which must arise from intemperate heats and irregular commotions." It could not be proved that Preston ordered his men to attack or shoot, and he was excused. However, two soldiers were found guilty of murder. This did not help the relationship between Britain and the colonists.

4. From Teacher to Soldier

Samuel Adams led another town meeting after the Boston Massacre in 1770. This one called for the formation of committees of correspondence in each colony that would help all the colonies to stay in touch with one another. It allowed the colonies to exchange ideas and discuss plans, and to support one another in their struggle with Britain. When Nathan Hale was at Yale, students received news and information through the committees. The committees played an important part in bringing the colonists together in preparation for war with Britain.

The Boston Tea Party, in 1773, was another key event in British taxation. The East India Company, a British trading company, was having money problems. To help them with the sale of their tea to the colonists, Parliament passed the Tea Act. Before the Tea Act, merchants purchased tea from companies and then sold it at a higher price to the colonists. The Tea Act allowed the East India Company to sell directly to the colonists at a lower price, causing tea merchants to lose business.

This is the British East India Company seal.

As early as the 1600s, European trade companies, such as the East India Company, had set up outposts and colonies in various parts of the world. The companies transported goods such as sugar, rum, fur, and timber between their numerous outposts. West Africa was an important destination for European trade companies. Here natives of West Africa who had been enslaved could be bought and then sold to people in places all over the world. Enslaved Africans were brought to America in the 1600s, and they became an integral part of America. By the time of the American Revolution, the slave-trading business had become an important part of the economy in the colonies. However, it challenged the ideas at hand: independence and self-rule. The topic of slavery was fiercely debated among the founding fathers, and it would not be resolved until the 1800s with the Civil War.

However, the colonists would still have to pay a tax on the tea. In spite of the tax, the price of the tea was lower than tea from other companies that sold to the colonists. The Tea Act was intended to persuade the colonists to buy only British tea.

The colonists did not like this arrangement. They feared that if Parliament could control the sale of tea, it might interfere with other businesses, too. Where would British control end? In addition, although the East India Company tea cost less than the others, the tax angered the colonists. Because they had no voice in Parliament, they did not feel Britain should tax them.

The Sons of Liberty decided to do something. A group of them met the first tea ship, the *Dartmouth*, when it sailed into Boston Harbor in November 1773. The Sons of Liberty told the captain that the tea could not be unloaded and that it would have to be returned to Britain. He agreed. However, the governor of Massachusetts, Thomas Hutchinson, did not want the Sons of Liberty to rule the harbor. He refused to let the ship leave. The Sons of Liberty then posted a guard at the dock to make sure that no tea was unloaded. The ship had twenty days to pay its tax on the tea, which could only be done if the cargo was unloaded and sold. By December 16, the tea still had not been unloaded, so the ship would have to return to England.

The evening before the ship was to return, there was a meeting at the Old South Church. Once again,

This undated Currier lithograph shows the Boston Tea Party
of December 16, 1773. The men in the boat were patriots dressed
as Mohawk Indians. In protest against a tax on tea, they threw
the contents of 342 chests of tea into Boston Harbor, while the
citizens of Boston cheered them on. The British punished
the colonists with the Coercive, or Intolerable, Acts.

Samuel Adams spoke out: "This meeting can do nothing
more to save the country." This was the signal for which
the crowd was waiting. They departed the church and
went to the dock where the British ship was anchored.
Then men disguised themselves as Mohawk Indians,
boarded the ship, and dumped 342 chests of tea into the
harbor. The harbor was like one big pot of tea! It became
the ultimate symbol of colonial resistance. There were
similar revolts in New York and Philadelphia, but there
the tea ships were not even allowed into the harbors.
They were sent back to England.

Naturally the British were enraged at the loss of thousands of dollars' worth of tea. They passed the Coercive Acts to punish the Massachusetts colony. In the first Coercive Act, Parliament closed Boston Harbor effective until the city paid for the tea. This was a severe hardship because the city depended on the port for goods that people needed to live. The second Act placed the colony's government under military watch, and the people were not allowed to meet. The final two Acts provided support to the British soldiers who were keeping watch over the colonists. The colonists then had to provide food and shelter for the British solders. Finally, if a British soldier harmed a colonist while performing his duties, he could return to England for a hearing or trial. He did not have to be tried in the colonies. The colonists despised all of these burdens. They called them the Intolerable Acts, a threat to the self-rule they sought.

By the time Nathan Hale began his permanent teaching position in 1774, things had really heated up between the colonists and Parliament. Virginia, competing with Massachusetts as leader in the resistance, suggested all colonies meet to submit a combined protest against Britain. In September, this First Continental Congress met in Philadelphia. All colonies except Georgia sent delegates. The delegates were divided into two main groups, the rebels from Massachusetts and Virginia and the moderates from the middle colonies. After much discussion and debate, they agreed to declare the rights of the

This undated engraving by T. J. Augustus shows Patrick Henry and other delegates to the First Continental Congress, which met in 1774. The Congress, among other things, decided to boycott British goods until Britain repealed the Coercive Acts. Patrick Henry, standing at center, made several famous speeches that inspired America to fight for independence.

colonists and demand that Britain reverse the Intolerable Acts. Speaking with one voice, rather than as separate colonies, they hoped to convince the king. The Congress also voted to prohibit British goods from being imported to America, and American goods from being exported to Britain. The Congress wanted Britain to recognize the rights of the colonists. They had taken their first steps down the road to independence from Britain.

Patriots were pleased by the Congress's accomplishments. Its momentum remained strong all winter. In spring 1775, New England began to form a group of armed "minutemen." Minutemen were handpicked men from the militia. They were trained to be ready at a moment's notice. The British army controlled Boston, so the militia began quietly scouting every village in the outskirts of the city for supplies, arms, and gunpowder. The British army, suspicious of what was going on, headed into the Massachusetts countryside to find out where colonial weapons were stored.

Paul Revere, a Boston silversmith, and William Dawes rode quickly and quietly on horseback to Lexington in the middle of the night, alerting the minutemen and militia that the British would soon arrive. When the British reached Lexington on April 19, 1775, looking for hidden guns and gunpowder, the community was prepared. At daybreak seventy militiamen met on a meadow. The British and the militia spotted each other across the field. It was a fearful moment. All of a sudden, a shot was heard. No one knew who fired it. Because it signaled the start of a war, it has been called the shot heard 'round the world. The British then fired at the militia, who returned fire and then fled to nearby Concord, Massachusetts. Eight minutemen were killed and ten were wounded. At Concord, the British met more farmers who were armed and ready. More shots were fired, with losses to both sides. The British continued to lose men as the army retreated back to Boston. The Americans, who lay in ambush to attack the

This statue of a minuteman stands in Lexington Green, part of Minuteman National Historical Park. The statue was created in 1875, by Daniel Chester French. Cast from ten old cannons, the bronze statue shows a man with a musket in one hand and a coat and plow in the other. This represents the New England farmers who took up the fight for independence.

Paul Revere became a legendary Revolutionary War hero after he warned his fellow patriots about the arrival of British troops. His ride to Lexington was immortalized in a famous ballad by the author Henry Wadsworth Longfellow. He would also carry word of the battle to the other colonies, like New York and Philadelphia.

British soldiers, easily spotted their bright red coats against the dark trees. These events marked the beginning of the American Revolution.

A messenger on horseback carried news of the battles at Lexington and Concord down the coast. He reached New London on April 21, and he aroused much excitement. A town meeting was called, and Nathan Hale spoke. Full of hope and promise, he wanted to march immediately. After the meeting, he volunteered for his local military force, the Connecticut militia, and men from New London formed a company. When the

Amos Doolittle made this handcolored engraving of the Battle of Lexington based on eyewitness accounts. The first of four panels that illustrate key events in Lexington and Concord on April 19, 1775, this sketch shows where the British and American soldiers were positioned when the first shots of the war were fired.

company marched immediately to assist around Boston, Hale stayed behind. Probably at the time he had no thought of really having to fight a British army. Until the war actually began, most people had expected a peaceful settlement. What would happen if the war continued? He had begun to think about his responsibility to his students. The war held a lot of uncertainties for the colonists. Nathan Hale felt confused about his duties. Should he continue to teach, or should he join the fighting himself?

In early July, Nathan Hale received a letter from his good friend Benjamin Tallmadge, who was also a teacher. Tallmadge was also unsure about fighting in the war. He had gone to Cambridge, Massachusetts, near Boston, to see for himself what was happening. He was deeply inspired by the enthusiasm of the Continental army. After his return home, Tallmadge wrote Hale, "Was I in your condition, I think the more extensive Service would be my choice. Our holy Religion, the honour of our God, a glorious country, & a happy constitution is what we have to defend."

The letter moved Hale. He believed in the patriot cause. With great regret, he withdrew from teaching and joined the militia full-time. He was appointed as

Among the various ranks within the Continental army, that of general was the highest. The commander in chief of the entire army was General George Washington, but Washington had other generals who assisted him. Other officers, in order of descending rank, were colonels, lieutenant colonels, majors, captains, lieutenants, sergeant majors, sergeants, and corporals. Nathan was appointed lieutenant in Webb's regiment, but he was later promoted to captain.

lieutenant in Colonel Charles Webb's Seventh Regiment. Nathan Hale stopped in New Haven for a last visit and talked to friends about the importance of the war and the need for soldiers. He even enlisted a few men for his company. He then marched with his company to Cambridge, where General George Washington was camped. The departure of the young men left many colonists uneasy. How would this war work out? The British had a powerful army. The patriot army was just assembling and had few weapons and little money. Yet the colonists were determined, especially Nathan Hale, whose devotion to his country would be his legacy.

5. Hale Takes Action for the Patriot Cause

Before Nathan Hale reached Boston, the British seized the southern area near its harbor in an effort to recapture the city. They were frustrated that the colonists were able to take the higher ground on the north side of the city at Breed's Hill. In June 1775, British General Thomas Gage decided to drive out the Americans. He succeeded, but at great cost. The Americans lost almost four hundred men, either dead or wounded, but the British lost more than a thousand. This battle has gone down in history as the Battle of Bunker Hill. The British government reacted with outrage to news of the battle. On August 23, King George III declared New England in a state of resistance to the Crown. Nevertheless, many ordinary British people, and even some members of Parliament, took the American side.

Following the Battle of Bunker Hill, the Virginian George Washington, veteran of the French and Indian War, led the Continental army in a standoff with British troops. Washington knew a fight was ahead, and that his army was in great need of supplies and

This picture, based on a copper engraving by J. Baker published in 1832, shows the Battle of Bunker Hill. This battle, which actually took place on Breed's Hill, occurred on June 17, 1775. It was a close battle and many lives were lost on both sides, but the colonists were forced to retreat when they ran out of ammunition.

heavy artillery. In November, he ordered Colonel Henry Knox to march on Fort Ticonderoga in upstate New York, then occupied by the British. Because the British at the fort had not yet learned of the fighting at Lexington and Concord, the colonials captured the fort with ease, and took the cannons. Through winter cold and frozen terrain, they dragged the cannons to Boston. Having accomplished this incredible feat, the exhausted soldiers arrived in Boston in January 1776.

Washington ordered Nathan's company to camp at the foot of Winter Hill, to the left of Washington's main force. From this post, they guarded the two roads by which the British could escape the city. It was here that Washington had trained the militia and had formed them into an army. Yet it was difficult for Washington to maintain his army over the course of the winter. With no united American government to conduct a draft, when times got tough, or when their short commissions ended, men simply quit the army and went home. Nathan Hale, however, took his role as soldier seriously and threw himself into his duties. He made every attempt to be the best officer he could. He encouraged his fellow soldiers to continue to serve.

This 1795 painting, titled *George Washington Reviewing the Western Army at Fort Cumberland, Maryland,* is by Frederick Kemmelmeyer, who witnessed the event. Throughout the Revolutionary War, Washington was commander in chief of the army. This scene shows a typical duty he would have performed before many of the major battles of the war.

This is a bronze statue of Nathan Hale by Enoch S. Woods from 1889. It is located at the Wadsworth Atheneum Museum of Art, in Hartford, Connecticut.

He even offered to give his own pay to men in his company whose service had expired, if they would stay. Although he wished he could see more battle activity himself, Nathan Hale remained true to the patriot cause.

During this time, Hale went back to Coventry, Connecticut, to enlist more soldiers from among his former schoolmates. After a month at home, he returned with fresh recruits. On January 30, 1776, Nathan's regiment was sent to the Dorchester peninsula, just south of Boston. They had chosen the peninsula as the place to set up the cannons that Colonel Knox's men had brought back from Fort Ticonderoga. With this move, Washington had put the British in an undefendable position. Without warning, the British fled north to Canada, taking a thousand Tories with them. Although for the moment the patriot forces had won Boston, the British force was reorganizing and was being strengthened in Canada.

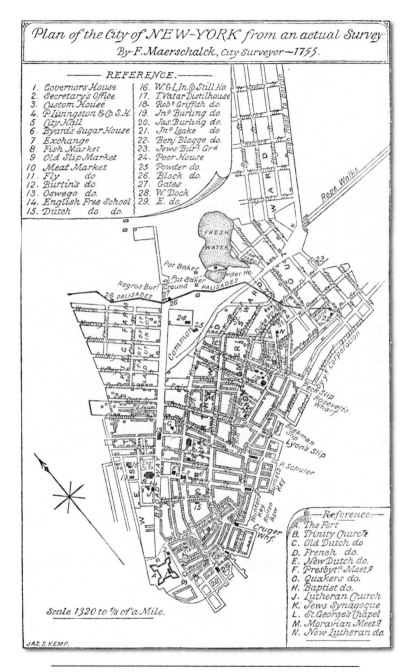

Plan of the City of NEW-YORK from an actual Survey
By F. Maerschalck, City Surveyor—1755.

——— REFERENCE. ———

1. Governors House
2. Secretary's Office
3. Custom House
4. P. Livingston & Co. S.H.
5. City Hall
6. Byard's Sugar House
7. Exchange
8. Fish Market
9. Old Slip Market
10. Meat Market
11. Fly do
12. Burtin's do
13. Oswego do.
14. English Free School
15. Dutch do. do.

16. W. & L. In. @ Still Ho.
17. T. Vatar Distilhouse
18. Robt Griffith do.
19. Jno Burling do.
20. Jas. Burling do.
21. Jno Leake do
22. Benj Blagge do.
23. Jews Burl Grd
24. Poor House
25. Powder do.
26. Block do.
27. Gates
28. W. Dock
29. E. do.

——— Reference: ———

A. The Fort
B. Trinity Church
C. Old Dutch do
D. French do.
E. New Dutch do.
F. Presbytn Meetg
G. Quakers do.
H. Baptist do.
J. Lutheran Church
K. Jews Synagogue
L. St. George's Chapel
M. Moravian Meetg
N. New Lutheran do.

Scale 1320 to ⅛ of a Mile.

JAS. S. KEMP.

This is a plan of New York City, showing the tip of Manhattan, which was developed, and the undeveloped farmland up to about present-day 42nd Street. B. Ratzen created this map in 1766 and 1767, based on his own surveys and surveys done in 1755 by the city surveyor. After the British left Boston, Washington believed that they would focus their next attack on New York.

Washington believed that the British army's next point of attack would be New York City, then located only in lower Manhattan. (The rest of Manhattan Island was undeveloped land.) Most people believed that the strategic location of New York on the Hudson would give whoever held it the upper hand in the war. That is where Washington sent his army, including Webb's regiment, and with it Nathan Hale's company. They marched to New London and then went by boat to New York. Hale spent six months in New York, building fortifications and preparing for an eventual battle.

The colonists were disturbed by the death and destruction caused by the war. Was it worth losing so many lives and risking punishment from the king? In January 1776, an Englishman who had immigrated to America two years earlier published a pamphlet called *Common Sense*. His name was Thomas Paine and his was the voice for which Americans had been waiting. He said America could be a new and different country. He wrote that a monarchy, a form of government led by a king, was a threat to American rights. Some people believed that the problem for the American colonies was the politicians in Parliament. Paine believed that the colonies would never achieve self-government as long as there was a king, an empire, and a monarchy. He also believed that the colonies did not need Britain for economic growth. He wrote, "The commerce by which she [America] hath

This is an engraved portrait of Thomas Paine by William Sharp.
Paine was born in Thetford, England, and he worked as a staymaker
and tax collector before coming to America and finding
work as a writer for *Pennsylvania Magazine*. Later he would write
several best-selling pamphlets in America and Europe,
arguing for independence and democracy.

enriched herself are the necessaries of life, and will always have a market while eating is the custom of Europe." He believed that the colonists had already showed a great commitment to independence, and he encouraged the fight forward: "We have it in our power to begin the world over again. A situation, similar to the present, hath not happened since the days of Noah until now." *Common Sense* sold more than one hundred thousand copies in January 1776, equal to about fifteen million today. Paine's reflective and powerful words appeared at just the right time. His ideas inspired the colonists to support the Second Continental Congress, which had met several months earlier in May 1775. This meeting had been called to discuss a formal separation from England.

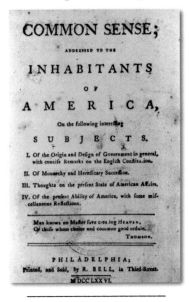

Published on January 10, 1776, *Common Sense*, a forty-seven-page pamphlet, sold out within two weeks.

The Second Continental Congress met in Philadelphia. With the war already under way, the colonists had no official document stating their views. The war was advancing. How could the colonies organize their army? There were no laws in place to bring order during this tense and chaotic time. As in the

First Continental Congress of 1774, delegates represented each colony. Some were fearful of cutting ties with England, and they worried about how the weak and inexperienced army would carry on against the powerful British with their large navy. The colonists could suffer a bloody defeat. Indeed, this seemed likely to happen. Even if they won, how could the colonies take care of themselves without the aid of a mighty empire, like England? For weeks, the delegates debated heatedly to find a resolution.

Finally, on June 7, 1776, Richard Henry Lee from Virginia voiced a daring idea: "These colonies are and of right ought to be free and independent states." If Lee's idea was accepted, the states would need a central government to carry on the war. Two committees were formed, one to draft a document claiming independence and another to prepare the articles, or laws, by which this new government would operate. On July 4 of that same year, the eloquent Declaration of Independence, written mainly by Thomas Jefferson of Virginia, was adopted.

The Declaration of Independence declared officially that the aim of the fighting was independence from the mother country, England. It claimed that people have the right to ". . . life, liberty, and the pursuit of happiness; that, to secure these rights, governments are instituted among men, deriving their just powers from the consent of the governed; that whenever any form of

Richard Henry Lee lived from 1732 to 1794. He was a signer of the
Declaration of Independence. Lee distrusted a strong national
government, fearing that the individual states would lose rights and
power. Feeling that the Constitution did not protect people's rights, he
worked against its ratification until a Bill of Rights was adopted in 1791.

government becomes destructive of these ends, it is the right of the people to alter or to abolish it . . ."

Until this time, many Americans believed the conflict could be resolved. This new declaration was a turning point for the colonists. It forced people to choose sides. Those who remained loyal to the king, the loyalists or Tories, were considered a threat to American security. They were made outcasts by the patriots. Many Tories were jailed and their property was taken and was sold to pay for the war. Some escaped to Canada, and still others kept silent until the arrival of the British army enabled them to reveal their beliefs. Tories also enlisted with the British army. Some families were split apart.

On July 9, 1776, a copy of the Declaration of Independence was read publicly in New York. The reading inspired patriots to pull down a statue of King George III in protest. The statue, located at Bowling Green in Manhattan, was made of lead and portrayed the king seated on his horse. After pulling down the statue, the patriots carted away pieces of it. The lead was later melted down to make bullets to use against the British.

This is the Declaration of Independence, written by Thomas Jefferson in 1776. It is the most cherished symbol of liberty in America. The political ideas in the declaration were not new, though, having been expressed by philosophers like John Locke. Jefferson simply summarized these ideas as "self-evident truths" and then listed the colonies' complaints against the king to justify their desire to break from Britain.

During the Revolutionary War, the colonies bonded together to separate from England. Once the war was over in 1783, the colonies went back to having separate governments. America was like thirteen separate countries in one. As the colonies started to do business with each other, there was no official law to give order or help solve problems. Finally, in 1787, the Continental Congress was called to Philadelphia to address these problems. The country needed a unifying voice. That voice would be the U.S. Constitution. The colonists had concerns, however. Why did they have to become one nation? They feared that the leaders unifying the government would take control over them, threatening the independence the war had won them. The founding fathers had similar concerns, and so the Bill of Rights was added to the Constitution, ensuring individual liberties for the people.

Not everyone took sides, though. Many feared the radicals on both sides and disliked all the upheaval. Nathan was serving with Washington in New York when he learned of the Declaration of Independence. For Nathan Hale, the Declaration of Independence confirmed his belief in the patriot cause.

6. Hale Volunteers to Become a Spy

In August 1776, the British invaded Brooklyn, across the East River from Manhattan Island. The fighting there, known as the Battle of Long Island, was a disaster for the Continental army. They barely survived by retreating to Manhattan through a heavy fog. The colonial army was dangerously encamped in the north of Manhattan, in Harlem Heights, facing a much better trained and supplied army.

At this point, Hale had been in the army for a year. He had not fought during the Battle of Long Island because his regiment's positions were never attacked. Nathan Hale's work had consisted mostly of keeping records and supervising guard duty. However, it has been said that he captured a small British vessel loaded with supplies. Hale led a brave night assault, taking the much-needed goods.

Nathan Hale had also been selected to serve in a special corps of rangers. This corps, handpicked and commanded by Lieutenant Colonel Thomas Knowlton, was called Congress' Own or Knowlton's Rangers. They were scouts. Their mission was to keep a close watch on

This hand-colored engraving of the Battle of Long Island by
James Smillie is based on a painting by Alonzo Chappel.
The August 1776 battle was a disaster for the American soldiers,
and they are shown here retreating from the British troops.

the British lines around New York and to gather information about the enemy's movements. By this time,
Nathan Hale had been promoted to the rank of captain.
In early September 1776, General Washington made an
urgent request to Lieutenant Colonel Knowlton for a
capable man to perform a daring assignment.

The situation looked grim for the Continental army.
The troops were suffering in many ways. The men were
in low spirits, discouraged by defeat at the Battle of
Long Island. They had lost confidence. Many were sick

and were deserting the army. Cold weather was approaching, but clothing, blankets, and tents were in short supply. Although soldiers were supposed to be paid, there was no money to pay them.

The British army was in much better shape. They far outnumbered the American troops and were better supplied with food, warm clothing, weapons, ammunition, and shelter. The British were also backed by a powerful navy, which guarded the waters surrounding Manhattan. The victorious British army now occupied Long Island. Hoping desperately to defend the island of Manhattan from attack, General Washington and what was left of the continental army were camped in Harlem Heights.

During the Revolution, both the British and the Americans tried to influence the local Indian groups throughout the colonies. The British wanted them to join the king's cause and help the British army by attacking American settlements. The British had had strong ties with many of the tribes, especially the powerful Iroquois, since the French and Indian War. The Americans, however, urged the Indians to stay neutral. They said the war was between England and the colonies—there was no need for the Indians to get involved. As might be expected, some of the native groups sided with the British and others with the Americans.

This is an undated engraving of George Clinton, who lived from 1739 to 1812. During the Revolution, Clinton was in charge of the defense of the Hudson River Valley. Later Clinton served seven times as governor of New York and was twice elected vice president of the United States.

Washington was worried. He was not sure what action to take because he did not know what the British would do next. Would they attack Manhattan directly? If so, where? Would they station troops on the far side of the Harlem and East Rivers, cutting off communication between the American troops and the mainland? New York was a prime strategic location. Its deep harbor was an excellent place for the large British navy to station its ships. Its rivers led into the country's interior, where the Americans were camped. Whoever controlled New York was in a strong position to win the war.

Washington asked his generals, William Heath and George Clinton, to create a "channel of information" to find out what the British were planning. He wrote to Heath: "Leave no stone unturned, nor do not stick at expense to bring this to pass, as I never was more uneasy than on account of my want of knowledge on this score. Keep constant lookout, with good glasses, on some commanding heights that look well on to the other shore."

Washington also had to decide whether to abandon the city. New York's population was mostly loyal to the British government. Did it make sense to defend a city that was on the verge of being invaded and whose inhabitants mostly would welcome the British? If the American troops did retreat from the city, should they burn it before they left so the British troops would have no place to stay for the winter? Washington asked

Congress what should be done. Congress was against burning the city. Its answer to Washington was that if the American troops did abandon New York, Washington should "have special care taken that no damage be done to the city" because Congress was sure it could be retaken at a later time. After holding a council of war with his officers, General Washington ordered that the troops remain in New York to defend it.

Washington still had no idea what the British were planning. Generals Heath and Clinton were unable to get any useful information. Washington was becoming desperate. He had hoped the generals could find a patriot willing to volunteer as a spy, but no one volunteered. He was even willing to have the generals find a Tory who could be bribed to spy on the British "for a reasonable reward," but that too failed. Finally Washington asked Lieutenant Colonel Knowlton to seek out a volunteer from among his rangers. This man would, in disguise, cross over the British lines on Long Island and would gather information in the enemy's camps. He would have to be trustworthy and courageous, an educated man with military experience who was cautious and used good judgment.

Knowlton called a meeting of his officers and asked for a volunteer, as no one could be ordered to be a spy. All were silent. No one wanted the assignment. It was not just the danger of the mission that caused them to refuse. These men were patriots and risked their lives

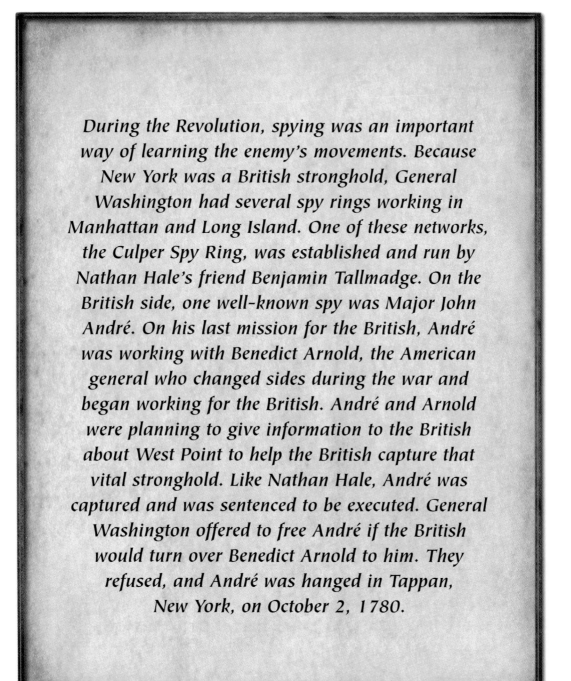

During the Revolution, spying was an important way of learning the enemy's movements. Because New York was a British stronghold, General Washington had several spy rings working in Manhattan and Long Island. One of these networks, the Culper Spy Ring, was established and run by Nathan Hale's friend Benjamin Tallmadge. On the British side, one well-known spy was Major John André. On his last mission for the British, André was working with Benedict Arnold, the American general who changed sides during the war and began working for the British. André and Arnold were planning to give information to the British about West Point to help the British capture that vital stronghold. Like Nathan Hale, André was captured and was sentenced to be executed. General Washington offered to free André if the British would turn over Benedict Arnold to him. They refused, and André was hanged in Tappan, New York, on October 2, 1780.

daily to fight for American independence, but no one wanted to become a spy. Spying was considered a dishonorable act. If caught, a spy was executed in what was considered a shameful manner: He was hanged rather than shot.

Despite these factors, one person did volunteer—Captain Nathan Hale. He surprised his comrades. They knew him well and admired him, and they did not want to see him risk his life that way. Nonetheless, Nathan Hale was eager to help win the war in any way he could. He felt he was not doing enough for the cause of liberty and was willing to take the risk. Hale was convinced that slipping into the British camps in disguise was the only way to get the information Washington needed. He felt there was no dishonor in doing what had to be done. "Every kind of service necessary for the public good becomes honorable by being necessary," he told a fellow officer and good friend, Captain William Hull. The two men had attended Yale together.

In a memoir published in 1848, Hull wrote that Nathan Hale came to see him after the meeting of Knowlton's officers. Hale asked his friend's opinion about what he had volunteered to do. Hull was distressed. He told Hale that he was sure the mission would be unsuccessful and that Hale's "short, bright career" would end with his execution. Hull tried in vain to talk Nathan Hale out of his decision, pointing out that he did not have the character of a spy. Hull told

Hale that "his nature was too frank and open for deceit and disguise, and he was incapable of acting a part equally foreign to his feelings and habits."

According to Hull, Nathan Hale replied by saying, "I am fully sensible of the consequences of discovery and capture in such a situation. But for a year I have been attached to the army and have not rendered any material service, while receiving a compensation for which I make no return . . . I wish to be useful."

Hull urged him to reconsider, but Nathan Hale held firm. He took his friend's hand and said, "I will reflect, and do nothing but what duty demands." Shortly afterward Hale left for the British lines, and Hull never saw him again.

7. Hale Undertakes His Mission

Nathan Hale's orders were to cross Long Island Sound, the body of water between the northern coast of Long Island and the mainland. After being left on shore on Long Island, Hale was to make his way into the British camps. He carried a general order directing the captain of any American ship to take him to whichever point on Long Island that he chose. First, however, he had to find a safe place from which to sail. On about September 12, Nathan Hale left the camp at Harlem Heights with his friend Stephen Hempstead, a sergeant under Hale's command. The two men planned to cross the sound the first chance they got. They went all the way to Norwalk, Connecticut, 50 miles (80.5 km) east of New York, and there, on September 15 or 16, set sail on the sloop *Schuyler* under the command of Captain Charles Pond.

When the *Schuyler* dropped off Nathan on the shore of Huntington Bay on Long Island, he had changed from his uniform into plain brown clothes and a wide-brimmed hat. Disguised as a Dutch schoolmaster, he

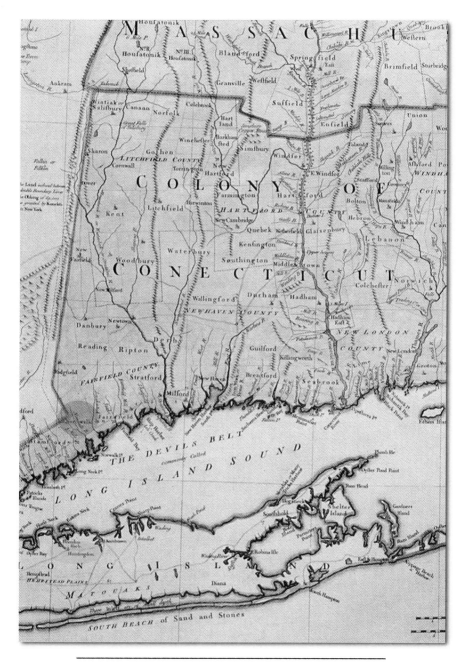

Nathan Hale crossed from Norwalk, Connecticut, highlighted in pink on the map, to Huntington Bay on Long Island, highlighted in blue. Hale would sneak behind the enemy lines disguised as a schoolmaster to gather information about British plans.

carried with him his diploma from Yale. It seemed a fitting costume, as he had been a teacher not long before. Nathan Hale gave his uniform, his silver buckles, and all of his papers, except the diploma, to Hempstead, along with instructions to wait for him to come back. Years later, in 1827, Sergeant Hempstead would write a letter to the editor of the newspaper the *St. Louis Republican*, in which he described the experience: "Thus equipped, we parted for the last time in life. He went on his mission, and I returned back again to Norwalk, with orders to stop there until he should return, or hear from him, as he expected to return back again to cross the sound, if he succeeded in his object." So Hempstead left on the *Schuyler* with Captain Pond and returned to Norwalk. It was the last he saw of Nathan Hale.

Although brave and full of enthusiasm, Nathan Hale had not been properly prepared for his mission by his superiors. He was not trained in the techniques of spying, and no cover story was created to explain why he was absent from camp. Therefore, this secret mission was not much of a secret. Information about his movements could easily have been leaked to the enemy. Nor was he given invisible ink, which had been invented several years earlier, with which to take his notes. Besides these disadvantages, Hale stood out physically: He was very tall and had a scar on his face from exploding gunpowder. He also had a Tory cousin who could

This is the letter that Stephen Hempstead wrote to the *St. Louis Republican* on January 27, 1827. In it he wrote of his last meeting with Nathan Hale and of the mission Hale was about to undertake.

This is an undated watercolor of Nathan Hale by R. Sterling Heraty.

have recognized him. Yet Nathan Hale managed to blend in undetected with the British for some time. Hale claimed he was a teacher looking for work, and a true loyalist to the British government. Without arousing any suspicion, he visited the British camps on Long Island. While in the camps, Nathan Hale was able to take notes in Latin and make sketches of British fortifications, which he hid in the soles of his shoes.

On September 15, 1776, around the time Nathan Hale arrived on Long Island, the British landed in lower Manhattan at Kips Bay on the East River and seized the city. Nathan Hale's mission had been to gather information about this plan of attack. However, by the time he had arrived on Long Island, the British had already succeeded. Although the British were then in possession of New York City, Nathan continued to gather information about their movements.

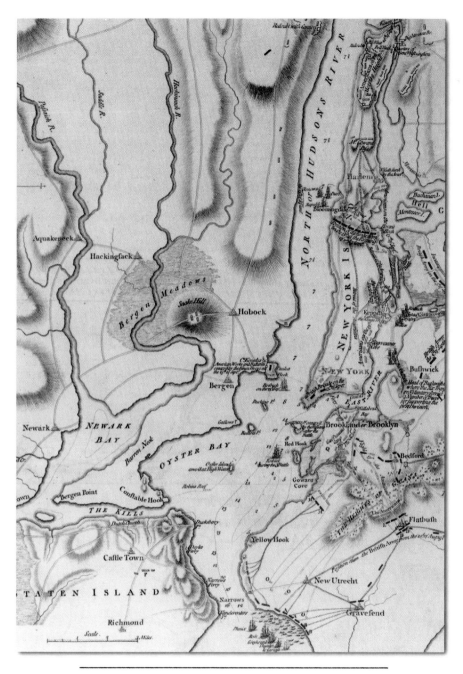

This is a late eighteenth-century map of New York. Kips Bay (spelled Kepps Bay on the map) is highlighted in yellow. On September 15, 1776, the British landed at Kips Bay on the East River and took over New York City.

Nathan was captured on September 21. Where he was captured is not known for certain, although it probably happened in Manhattan. Some accounts say it was on the shores of Huntington, Long Island, where a boat from the British warship *Halifax* picked him up. According to this story, Nathan mistook the *Halifax* as his rescue boat, coming to pick him up after the completion of his assignment. However, according to the ship's log, the *Halifax* was not at Huntington on the night of September 21. It was at City Island, 25 miles (40.2 km) away. Nathan may have been captured close to the American lines in upper Manhattan, or maybe the western end of Long Island.

What happened to cause his capture? Why did the British suspect him? According to some accounts, Nathan was betrayed by his Tory cousin, Samuel Hale, who recognized him, assumed he was spying, and reported him to the British authorities. Samuel Hale denied it, and there is no historical evidence to prove this story. Captain Hull and Nathan's brother Enoch thought that he was captured because the British became suspicious of his behavior.

The British would have been overly suspicious of anyone on the day Nathan was captured, because something unexpected and disastrous for the British had happened. A great, destructive fire broke out in New York. How the fire began is still a mystery. Maybe it was deliberately set, or maybe it was an accident. The British blamed the

This modern-day French engraving shows the burning of New York City during the night of September 20, 1776. Though Washington was specifically told by Congress to spare the city, the British believed the fire was set on purpose, possibly at Washington's order. If it hadn't been for the heightened suspicion caused by the fire, Nathan Hale might never have been captured.

local patriots for setting it as an act of revenge against the British and their Tory allies. Some accounts claim that Nathan Hale himself was involved, although there is no evidence to support this. The fire caused panic among the people and destroyed nearly a quarter of the city. The angry British, blaming the Americans, rounded up many of them and threw them into the flames. In response to the fire, Washington said only, "Providence, or some good honest fellow, has done more for us than we were disposed to do for ourselves."

*In the early twentieth century,
archaeologists Reginald P. Bolton
and William L. Calver, excavating
in northern Manhattan, uncovered British
campsites from the Revolutionary War.
Some of the artifacts they found,
such as cannonballs, badges, bayonets,
and uniform buttons, reveal information
about a soldier's military life.
Other objects, such as scissors, keys,
combs, and smoking pipes, offer insights
into the more personal side of military
camp life. Soldiers, however, were not
the only ones who occupied Revolutionary
War camps. Women, most of them
soldiers' wives, cooked for the troops,
did the laundry, and nursed the
wounded. Toys excavated at the sites are
evidence that children, too, lived at camp.*

This undated engraving shows the Beekman Mansion, where Nathan Hale was brought after his capture on September 21, 1776. When the British took control of New York, the soldiers took up residence in the area's homes. This mansion, located near present-day 51st Street and First Avenue, was owned by the patriot James Beekman and was taken over by General William Howe.

Amid all of this confusion and mayhem, Nathan Hale was seized and was brought to the Beekman Mansion, located at Turtle Bay near present-day First Avenue and East 51st Street. This house, which once belonged to the patriot James Beekman, was the headquarters of the British commanding general, William Howe. Nathan, questioned by General Howe, could not deny he was a spy. When he had been searched, his notes and sketches had been found on him. Knowing he had been found out, Nathan Hale confessed and declared his name and army rank.

Nathan Hale was not given a trial. General Howe immediately ordered him hanged the next day. He was handed over to his jailer, Provost Marshal William Cunningham, a hard man who treated his prisoners cruelly. Under Cunningham's watch, Hale was taken to the greenhouse of the Beekman Mansion to await his execution.

8. Hale Is Executed

Captain John Montresor, a British officer and Howe's chief engineer, is the source of all that is known about what happened on the tragic Sunday morning of Hale's death. He would later, under a flag of truce, enter the American camp and would talk with Hale's friend and fellow officer, Captain Hull. Many years later, Hull would describe this visit in his memoirs. He told of how Montresor described Nathan Hale's imprisonment and execution, and that the British officer seemed moved by it.

This is a portrait of Captain John Montresor, a British officer who lived from 1736 to 1799.

According to Montresor, Hale had asked Cunningham to call a clergyman to be with him before his hanging, but Cunningham refused. Hale then asked for a Bible, but that request was refused, too. Montresor described Cunningham as a man "hardened to human suffering and every softening sentiment of the heart." Feeling sorry for the prisoner, Montresor invited Nathan Hale to sit awhile in the shelter of his tent while the hangman fixed the rope. Montresor told Hull that when Nathan Hale entered the tent "he was calm, and bore himself with gentle dignity."

Then Hale asked Montresor for writing materials to write two letters before he died. One was to his brother Enoch, the other to Colonel Knowlton. Hale was unaware that while he was away on his mission, Knowlton had been killed in battle. The letters were given to Cunningham, who did not deliver them and who may have destroyed them. A few months after Nathan Hale's death, his brother Enoch met Major John Palsgrave Wyllys, who was a British prisoner of war when Hale was caught. Wyllys told Enoch, who wrote about it in his diary, that Cunningham had shown him Nathan Hale's diploma and the two letters. Enoch had never received his letter and did not know about it until his talk with Wyllys.

Nathan Hale was hanged at 11:00 A.M. on Sunday, September 22, 1776, the morning after his capture. Where this took place has been a topic of debate for historians over the years. It was first thought that Hale was hanged near present-day City Hall Park in Manhattan. It was also once thought that he was executed on the site of the present-day United Nations. At the Yale Club, near Grand Central Terminal, there is a

Collection of the New-York Historical Society, Negative Number 505

This is a manuscript page from the orderly book, or diary, of a British officer who made mention of the execution of a spy on September 22, 1776. Historians believe that this spy was Nathan Hale, who had been captured the night before. William Kelby based his letter to the *New York Herald* (see page 85) on this diary, which he bought at an auction.

plaque stating that Nathan Hale was executed nearby. Other stories tell of his hanging occurring by an old ferry house in Brooklyn, and various other places in and around Manhattan.

Then, in 1893, William Kelby, librarian of The New-York Historical Society, wrote a letter to the *New York Herald* laying out evidence that Nathan was hanged near present-day Third Avenue and East 66th Street. Kelby had bought the diary of a British officer at an auction. In it, under the date of September 22, 1776, the officer had written: "A spy fm the Enemy (by his own full confession) apprehended Last Night, was this day Executed at 11 oClock in front of the Artillery Park." This would have been where the British "parked" their big guns, and Kelby set out to find where it was. His research placed it close to the Dove Tavern, "near the old five-mile stone, on the post road which led to Kingsbridge." That place is, today, Third Avenue near East 66th Street. It is now recognized as the most likely site of Nathan Hale's hanging. Where he is buried is still unknown. His body was probably placed in an unmarked grave near the place of execution.

Nathan Hale went to his death with dignity. According to the diary of another British officer,

---

Previous Spread: This handcolored engraving shows the execution of Nathan Hale on September 22, 1776. This woodcut ran in the 1860 *Harper's Weekly* newspaper in a series of illustrations designed to stop secession from the Union by stirring up patriotic feelings.

Collection of the New-York Historical Society, Negative Number 50381

This is the article written by William Kelby, librarian of the New-York Historical Society, in 1893. The article that would help place the site of Hale's execution was titled "Nathan Hale, the Patriot Spy," and ran in the *New York Herald*, on November 26, 1893, on page 3.

This is an eighteenth-century portrait of Joseph Addison.

Nathan Hale's famous last words remain a source of debate among historians. If Hale did say them, he was probably paraphrasing a line from the play Cato, *about a man's last stand for liberty against a tyrant. Hale, who enjoyed plays and acting, was familiar with this piece, written by Joseph Addison in 1713.*

How beautiful is death, when earn'd by virtue!
Who would not be that youth? What pity it is
That we can die but once to serve our country!
—*Cato, Act 4, Scene 4*

Lieutenant Frederick Mackenzie, Hale "behaved with great composure and resolution, saying he thought it the duty of every good Officer to obey any orders given him by his Commander-in-Chief; and desired the Spectators to be at all times prepared to meet death in whatever shape it might appear."

Nathan Hale was hanged either from a tree or a gallows made from a wooden frame, as was the practice in those days. The prisoner's hands were tied and he was forced to climb a ladder, which was then pulled out from under him. Hale's death was not attended by a large crowd. Montresor told Hull that there were only a few persons gathered around, "yet his characteristic dying words were remembered. He said, 'I regret that I have but one life to lose for my country.'" Unfortunately, these words were not published for many years, so it is not certain what it is he actually said—or if Captain Hull perhaps did not remember exactly what Captain Montresor told him.

9. The Patriot Remembered

When Captain Montresor crossed the American lines after Nathan Hale's execution, he was on an assignment to discuss a prisoner exchange. One of the officers he met was Hull, and it was through this meeting that Hull first learned of his friend's capture and execution. In fact, this was the first time that news of Nathan's capture and execution was known to the American side. His fate was never officially revealed by General Washington. Although Nathan Hale is a hero today, in 1776, his death was not an important event. Although loved by those who knew him, he was not honored in his time. His execution caused no outcry among the patriots. The American Revolution would not end until 1783, and Hale's death was overshadowed by the events of the war. Hale died quietly, and his body was never recovered.

The first time that the story of Nathan Hale appeared in publication was in 1799, in Hannah Adams's *A Summary History of New England and General Sketch of the American War*. Adams got her

This 1795 portrait of George Washington was painted by Gilbert Stuart. Washington, president from 1789 to 1797, was sixty-three at the time, and had no interest in sitting for his portrait. In fact, Stuart said Washington "was most apalling to paint." To make the paintings more interesting and lively, the artist used quick, sketchy brush strokes. Stuart also tried to indicate Washington's imposing six-foot, two-inch height by positioning his head high on the canvas.

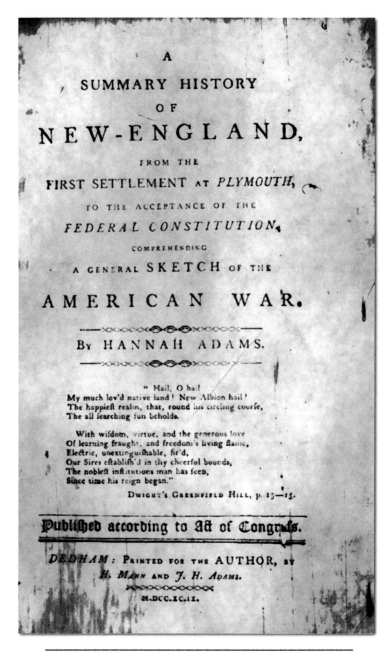

A

SUMMARY HISTORY

O F

NEW-ENGLAND,

FROM THE

FIRST SETTLEMENT AT *PLYMOUTH*,

TO THE ACCEPTANCE OF THE

FEDERAL CONSTITUTION,

COMPREHENDING

A GENERAL SKETCH OF THE

AMERICAN WAR.

BY HANNAH ADAMS.

" Hail, O hail
My much lov'd native land! New Albion hail!
The happiest realm, that, round his circling course,
The all searching sun beholds.

With wisdom, virtue, and the generous love
Of learning fraught, and freedom's living flame,
Electric, unextinguishable, fir'd,
Our Sires establish'd in thy cheerful bounds,
The noblest institutions man has seen,
Since time his reign began."

DWIGHT's GREENFIELD HILL, p. 13—15.

Published according to Act of Congress.

DEDHAM: PRINTED FOR THE AUTHOR, BY
H. MANN AND J. H. ADAMS.

M.DCC.XC.IX.

This is the title page of Hannah Adams's history of New England.
It was published in 1799, and was recorded for history. She based
her version of the story on information she received from
Captain Hull, Hale's friend.

information from Captain Hull. Other published accounts of the Revolution followed, but none mention Hale until 1824, when Adams's was reprinted in Jedediah Morse's *Annals of the American Revolution*. On January 27, 1827, Stephen Hempstead wrote his letter in the *St. Louis Republican*. Finally, in 1848, Captain Hull's daughter, Mrs. Mariah Campbell, published her father's memoirs. It is not known when Hull wrote them. It is from these memoirs that we

This portrait of Captain William Hull is credited to an artist named Sharples. It was painted between 1795 and 1800. Hull lived from 1753 to 1825. John Montresor would find Hull in the American camp, under a flag of truce, to tell him about Hale's execution. Hull wrote the tale down in his memoirs, which his daughter published in 1848.

have the firsthand accounts of his meeting with Hale after Hale volunteered to become a spy, and Hull's meeting with Montresor after Hale's hanging. Today the story of Nathan Hale is found in history books and school textbooks throughout the country. He is remembered as a national hero who symbolizes the spirit of American patriotism. Hale held to his beliefs until the end, when he lost his life for liberty.

Many statues and memorials have been raised in Hale's honor. In Huntington, Long Island, is the Nathan Hale Stone. An engraved plaque on the stone states that on this spot Nathan Hale was captured by

Collection of the New-York Historical Society, Negative Number 45406

This is the Nathan Hale Stone in Huntington Bay, Long Island, placed in 1897 by George Taylor. It was originally placed on the beach near where Hale began his mission but was moved inland. Many of the quotes on the stone are incorrect, or there is no evidence to back up their accuracy. For instance, the stone reads that Hale "was captured on this shore," but he was more likely caught in New York.

NATHAN HALE

LEGENDARY 21-YEAR OLD HERO OF
THE REVOLUTIONARY WAR WAS
HANGED AS AN AMERICAN SPY ON
SUNDAY, SEPTEMBER 22, 1776,
PROBABLY WITHIN 100 YARDS OF
HERE. ARRESTED SATURDAY NIGHT,
HE WAS INTERROGATED AND
SENTENCED BY THE BRITISH
COMMANDER. GENERAL WILLIAM
HOWE, AT HIS HEADQUARTERS NEAR
WHAT IS NOW THE UNITED NATIONS.
THE EXACT LOCATION OF THE
HANGING IS ONE OF HISTORY'S
UNCERTAINTIES. OTHER PLACES HAVE
BEEN CITED, BUT A BRITISH
OFFICER'S DIARY INDICATES THE
ROYAL ARTILLERY PARK NEAR THE
DOVE TAVERN ON THE OLD POST
ROAD, NOW THIRD AVENUE WHERE IT
INTERSECTS 66TH STREET.

THE NEW-YORK HISTORICAL SOCIETY WEBSITE HAS MORE DETAILS
WWW.NYHISTORY.ORG

Though there are several markers around New York City
claiming that Nathan Hale was hanged nearby, there is strong
evidence that the latest addition is the most accurate. Thanks to
the work of Richard Mooney, a plaque now hangs at Third Avenue
and East 66th Street. Its location is based on the orderly book
of a British officer, uncovered by historian William Kelby.

the British. Hale was probably not captured there, but historians agree that he landed there to begin his mission, and the stone stands as a tribute to his bravery.

A plaque commemorates the site where Hale was probably hanged, present-day Third Avenue and East 66th Street. The plaque is affixed to an apartment building, The Chatham, designed by Robert A. M. Stern—the dean of architecture at Yale, where Hale studied.

This is a silhouette of Nathan Hale. It was traced on the door
of the house where he was raised, in Coventry, Connecticut.
All the portraits and statues that have been created of Hale were
based on the descriptions of people from the time and this silhouette.

Although Nathan Hale never had his portrait painted, he has been described by people who knew him, and his profile, or silhouette, was traced on a door at his home in Coventry. Based on these descriptions, many statues have been created of the martyr patriot. Among the best known is the statue by Frederick MacMonnies that stands in the park at New York City Hall. The inscription reads, "Nathan Hale, a captain in the regular army of the United States who gave his life for his country in the city of New York, Sept. 22nd 1776," and also has the famous words "I regret that I have but one life to lose for my country."

Another well-known statue honoring Nathan Hale, sculpted by Bela Pratt, stands on the Yale campus outside Hale's dormitory, Connecticut Hall, which is still in use for student and faculty activity. A copy of Pratt's statue greets visitors to the headquarters of the Central Intelligence Agency (CIA) in Langley, Virginia. The CIA gathers information, or intelligence, about other countries that may affect our national safety, a task similar to the one that Nathan Hale took on during the Revolution.

In Coventry, the place of his birth, a monument dedicated to his memory was completed in 1846. It stands by the graveyard of the Congregational Church, near the graves of Hale's family members. Also in Coventry, the Hale Homestead—the farm where Nathan and his brothers and sisters grew up—survives as an historical

This statue of Nathan Hale, by Frederick MacMonnies, stands in City Hall Park in New York. An article about the statue's unveiling read, "In Bronze the Patriot Stands Where He Gave His Life for His Country." Nathan Hale actually was hanged far from here, but the statue is still a tribute to this legendary patriot.

landmark. The Connecticut Antiquarian and Landmarks Society owns and maintains the homestead, which is open to the public. Also, the schoolhouses where Hale taught in East Haddam and New London are still standing.

In visiting the many monuments and memorials to Nathan Hale, we are reminded of his important legacy. He is an American legend not so much for what he did, but rather because of the ideals for which he stood. Hale's fame is in his character. He willingly agreed to take on an assignment that he knew could end in death. His principles were so strong that he was unwavering in his performance of his duty. Steadfast until the end, he remained a loyal patriot even as he was led to his execution. Sacrificing his life

Though Nathan Hale's body has never been found, a monument honoring him has been erected near the graveyard of the Congregational Church in Coventry, Connecticut, where his family is buried.

This statue of Nathan Hale by Bela Pratt was erected in 1914. It stands outside Connecticut Hall, Nathan Hale's dormitory at Yale College. A copy of this famous statue also stands at the Central Intelligence Agency headquarters in Virginia.

for the cause of liberty, he stands as a symbol of determination and courage in the war for America's independence.

Although Hale did not complete his mission, the commitment of thousands of patriots like him eventually, and against all odds, achieved victory for the American cause. More than two hundred years later, amid the spirited streets of New York City, perhaps one in a thousand notices a small plaque paying tribute to a young man who bravely gave up his life for the birth of a new nation.

Timeline

1754	The French and Indian War begins.
1755	Nathan Hale is born.
1763	The Treaty of Paris is signed, ending the French and Indian War.
1764	The Sugar Act is passed by British parliament.
1765	The Stamp Act is passed by British parliament.
1769	Nathan Hale enters Yale College in New Haven, Connecticut.
1770	The Boston Massacre occurs.
	Committees of correspondence are formed.
1773	Nathan Hale graduates from Yale College.
	The Boston Tea Party occurs.

1774   Parliament passes the Coercive, or
        Intolerable, Acts on April 1, to punish the
        colonists for the Tea Party.

        Nathan Hale accepts a permanent teach-
        ing job in New London, Connecticut.

        The First Continental Congress meets in
        Philadelphia.

1775   Paul Revere makes his midnight ride to
        warn the countryside of British troop move-
        ments toward Lexington and Concord.

        The Battle of Lexington and Concord
        occurs, starting the Revolutionary War.

        The Second Continental Congress meets.

        Nathan Hale joins the militia full-time.

        The Battle of Bunker Hill occurs.

        In November, American troops march on
        Fort Ticonderoga and capture the fort
        from the British. Colonel Henry Knox and
        his men drag the cannons back to Boston.
        They arrive in Boston in January 1776.

Nathan Hale arrives in Boston and is assigned to the camp at Winter Hill.

1776   Nathan Hale returns to Coventry, Connecticut, to enlist men.

The British retreat from Boston, and Washington and his army, including Nathan Hale, head to New York.

In January, Thomas Paine's *Common Sense* is published.

In July, the Declaration of Independence is adopted.

Knowlton's Rangers is formed and Nathan Hale joins.

In August, the Battle of Long Island is fought.

In September, Nathan Hale accepts an assignment as a spy and is hanged less than two weeks later.

Glossary

agile (A-jul) Something that is able to move easily and gracefully.

benign (bih-NYN) Gentle.

boycott (BOY-kaht) A refusal to support something.

Coercive Acts (koh-ER-siv AKTS) The laws that British parliament passed to punish the colony of Massachusetts for the Boston Tea Party.

Continental army (kohn-tin-EN-tul AR-mee) The name of the American army during the Revolutionary War.

debate (dih-BAYT) A discussion between individuals or groups with different points of view, usually to determine which is to be followed.

delegate (DEH-lih-get) A person who presents ideas on behalf of many people.

democracy (dih-MAH-kruh-see) A system of government whereby people choose leaders and participate in making laws through an election process.

deportment (dih-PORT-mehnt) The way one carries oneself, or one's behavior.

effigy (EH-fuh-jee) A figure that represents a person.

empire (EM-pyr) A territory of land under the control of a monarch.

fraternity (fruh-TER-nuh-tee) A group of men who share a common interest.

gallows (GA-lohz) A structure from which a person is executed by hanging.

hallowed (HA-lohd) Respected or sacred.

independence (in-dih-PEN-dents) Freedom or self-rule.

Intolerable Acts (in-TOL-ruh-bul AKTS) The name the colonists gave to the Coercive Acts.

legislature (LEH-jus-lay-chur) The branch of government that makes laws.

loyalists (LOY-uh-lists) Colonists who supported British rule in America.

martyr (MAR-ter) Someone who willingly suffers, and often dies, for his or her beliefs.

militia (muh-LIH-shuh) A group of volunteer or citizen soldiers who are organized to assemble in emergencies.

minutemen (MIH-net-men) A group of militiamen trained to fight the British at a moment's notice during the American Revolution.

monarchy (MAH-nar-kee) A government ruled by a king or queen.

notable (NOH-tuh-bul) Standing out because of excellence or certain qualities.

Parliament (PAR-lih-mint) The British legislature.

patriots (PAY-tree-uhts) Colonists who believed in separating from British rule.

perseverance (per-suh-VEER-unts) Commitment and patience during a time of struggle.

radicals (RA-dih-kulz) People who have ideas that are not widely accepted and who express these ideas in extreme ways.

representation (reh-prih-zen-TAY-shun) The act of speaking on behalf of a person or group of people.

resistance (rih-ZIS-tents) A strong stand taken against something.

roseate (ROH-zee-et) Healthy, rosy complexioned.

Sons of Liberty (SUNZ UV LIH-ber-tee) An organization of radical patriots.

Stamp Act (STAMP AKT) The law British parliament passed that placed a tax on paper goods in the colonies.

Tea Act (TEE AKT) The law British parliament passed that allowed the British East India

Company to sell its tea directly to the colonists, causing tea merchants to lose business.

Tories (TOR-eez) Loyalists or colonists in support of British rule.

tyranny (TEER-uh-nee) A government with a single ruler who oppresses his or her people.

Whigs (WIGZ) Patriots or colonists who wanted separation from British rule.

Additional Resources

To learn more about Nathan Hale and the American Revolution, check out these books and Web sites.

Books

Crompton, Samuel Willard. *100 Colonial Leaders Who Shaped North America*. San Mateo, CA: Bluewood Books, 1999.

Lough, Loree. *Nathan Hale: Revolutionary Hero*. New York: Chelsea House Publishers, 1998.

Seymour, George Dudley. *Hale: Documentary Life of Nathan Hale, Comprising All Available Official and Private Documents Bearing on the Life of the Patriot*. Salem, MA: Higginson Book Company, 1995.

Web Sites

www.ctssar.org/patriots/nathan_hale.htm

www.lihistory.com/4/hs413a.htm

www.odci.gov/cia/ciakids/history/nathan.html

Bibliography

Bakeless, John. *Turncoats, Traitors and Heroes.* Philadelphia and New York: J. B. Lippincott Company, 1960.

Boatner, Mark. *Encyclopedia of the American Revolution.* New York: D. McKay Company, 1966.

Bryan, George S. *The Spy in America.* Philadelphia and New York: J. B. Lippincott Company, 1943.

Kelby, William. "Site of the Execution of Captain Nathan Hale." *The New-York Historical Society Quarterly* 2, no. 1 (April 1918): 8-13.

Lossing, Benson J. *The Two Spies: Nathan Hale and John André.* New York: D. Appleton and Company, 1886.

Pennypacker, Morton. *General Washington's Spies on Long Island and in New York.* Brooklyn, New York: The Long Island Historical Society, 1939.

Seymour, George Dudley. *Documentary Life of Nathan Hale.* New Haven: private printing for the author, 1941.

Shelton, William Henry. "What Was the Mission of Nathan Hale?" *Journal of American History* 9, no. 1, (1915): 269-289.

Index

About the Authors

L. J. Krizner is Director of Education at The New-York Historical Society in New York City. She develops programs in outreach education and integrates museum and classroom curriculum in a variety of American history topics. She has cocurated two exhibitions, *Kid City* and *$24: The Legendary Deal for Manhattan*. L. J. earned her Master's degree in museum education from Bank Street Teachers College in New York City. She also has recently published a book called *Peter Stuyvesant: New Amsterdam and the Origins of New York* with Lisa Sita.

Lisa Sita is Educational Programs Coordinator for The Luce Center for the Study of American Culture at The New-York Historical Society, where she teaches and develops programs about American history and society. She was co-curator of the New-York Historical Society exhibition *$24: The Legendary Deal for Manhattan* and has written several books for children on American Indian culture and other topics. Lisa holds undergraduate and Master's degrees in anthropology.

Credits

Photo Credits

Series Design

Laura Murawski

Layout Design

Corinne Jacob

Project Editor

Joanne Randolph

Photo Researcher

Jeffrey Wendt